What Makes This Sound?

Alan Trussell-Cullen

DOMINIE PRESS
Pearson Learning Group

ISBN 0-7685-0555-0

Printed in Singapore

10 11 12 VOZF 13 12 11 10 09

Dominie
Press

Pearson Learning Group

1-800-321-3106
www.pearsonlearning.com

Table of Contents

We hear sounds everywhere.

There are sounds all around us.

Some things make loud sounds.

What else makes loud sounds?

Some things make quiet sounds.

What else makes quiet sounds?

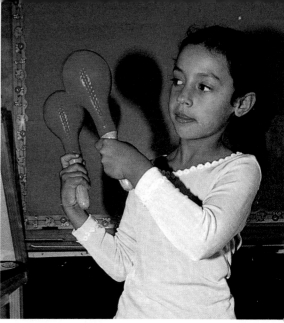

We can shake things

to make sounds.

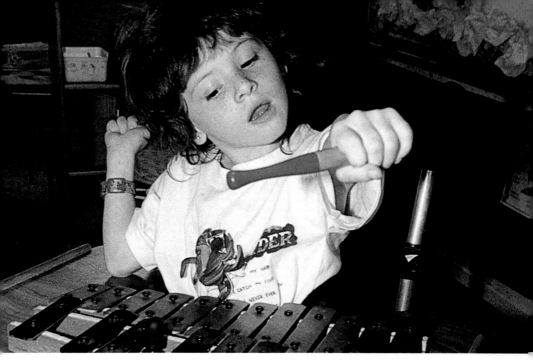

We can tap things

to make sounds.

We can pluck things

to make sounds.

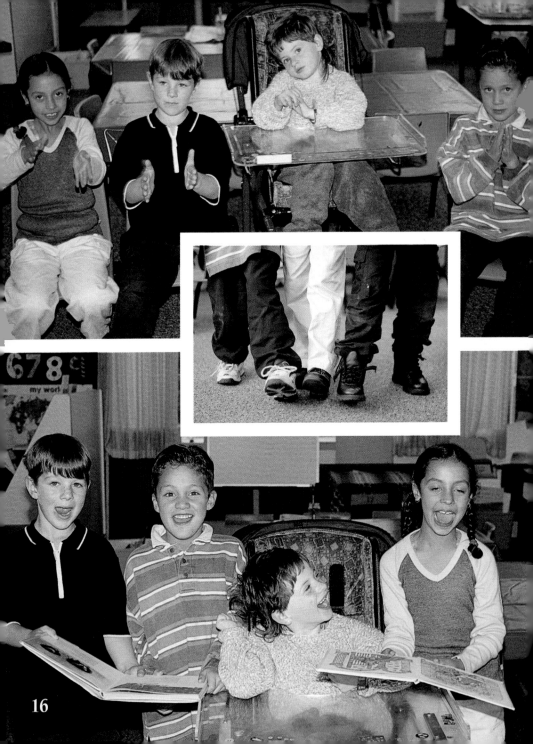

We can make sounds in other ways, too.

We can clap our hands.

We can tap our feet.

We can sing.

Picture Glossary

hands:

feet:

Index